How to Make a Book

homeschool edition

Shannon L Mokry

copyright

Copyright © 2024 Shannon L Mokry. All rights reserved.
Originally Copyrighted in 2020
You are welcome to print pages for your personal use.
Other than that, no part of this publication may be reproduced, stored, or transmitted in any form or by any means, electronic, mechanical, photocopying, recording, scanning, or otherwise, except as permitted under Section 107 or 108 of the 1976 United States Copyright Act, without the prior written permission of the author. Requests to the author and publisher for permission should be addressed to the following email: info@sillygeesepublishing.com

Limitation of liability/disclaimer of warranty: While the publisher and author have used their best efforts in preparing this guide, they make no representations or warranties with respect to the accuracy or completeness of the contents of this document and specifically disclaim any implied warranties of merchantability or fitness for particular purpose. No warranty may be created or extended by sales representatives, promoters, or written sales materials.

The advice and strategies contained herein may not be suitable for your situation. You should consult with a professional where appropriate. Neither the publisher nor author shall be liable for any loss of profit or any other commercial damages, including but not limited to special, incidental, consequential, or other damages.

Due to the dynamic nature of the Internet, certain links and website information contained in this publication may have changed. The author and publisher make no representations to the current accuracy of the web information shared.

ISBN: 9781951521936

dedication

I need to thank my husband for encouraging me and my youngest daughter for being such a willing helper in all my book efforts.

the author

Hi, my name is Shannon L. Mokry, and I'm a homeschooling mom and author. I studied Early Childhood Develop and English Studies during college, spent many years in the work force, then became a stay-at-home mom when my first daughter was born.

When I first became a Stay at Home mom, I had a book written, outlined, and ready to go, but I lacked the self confidence to follow through and get my book published. Fast forward fourteen years and God blessed me with new stories and a reason to pursue my passion. With three girls to raise, I needed to set a better example for them. I needed to live the life I wanted for each of them. A life not ruled by fear.

Maybe you have found yourself bound by fear, wanting more for your kids, yet unsure of how to accomplish that goal? That was once me. I learned that, not only is it important to live by example, but it is also important to help them develop the skills, and introduce them a variety of experiences, so that they are ready to follow their own dreams.

Shannon L. Mokry
www.sillygeesepublishing.com
www.facebook.com/shannonlmokry
www.instagram.com/whimsyandpurpose

How to Make a Book
homeschool kids edition

Buy this if you...

- Want to teach your child or class the process of making a book.
- Want to teach your child (truly basic) basic computer graphics skills.
- Want to make a keepsake.
- Want to showcase your child's art and writing skills - they grow so fast!

Plus many other reasons for making a book with the child or children or class. It can be a fun process if you let your child take the lead while you facilitate, helping as much or as little as your child needs. Remember the more you do the less it's your child's book.

Skip it if you...

- Want to make a book to sell commercially.
- Don't have the time to invest. This project will take us much commitment from you as it does the child.
- Want help marketing a book. I do not talk about marketing at all.

While I do cover some basic information for getting this book printed with a real printer, in no way am I suggestion that this ebook creates a professional quality book.

table of contents

Planning the Book .... page 7
Write It .... page 17
Story Starters .... page 20
Rewrite and Edit .... page 21
Illustration Time .... page 25
Finishing Touches ....page 29
Covers ....page 33
Story Board Pages .... page 37

step 1

Planning the Book

Plan it out

Set your student up for success

Let's start by agreeing on the end goal. In this book, the end goal is to have a complete book. For our purposes, that book will be a short picture book. We are looking to fill 24 pages, which includes a title page, a copyright page, and a dedication. One page is allowed if the author chooses to start the book on the right side of the page. I've included a mockup page builder at the end of the book to help with the process of planning. Take a moment now to find those pages. Then let's work our way through this list to plan out the best book possible.

- Purpose of book
- Type of book
- Genre of book
- Author page yes/no
- Outline of story
- Number of illustrations
- Size and shape of book (square or rectangle)

Purpose
Why are you doing this project?

Is it a keepsake, helping your child follow a passion, or a school assignment? All of these are valid, just be clear on your why.
My daughter has a vivid imagination and wants to be a writer, but doesn't want to read. Her book was a school assignment meant to give her a self esteem boost.
Every aspect was done with that last goal in mind.

Book Type
Picture book, graphic novel, or chapter book?

There are a lot of other options, but for the purposes of this guide we will focus on picture books. If your child wants to write a chapter book or novel, GREAT! You will still find some helpful tips, just pick and choose the parts that are useful to you. Graphic novels require stronger art talents, so refer to your favorite graphic novel for page setups you like.

Genre

What is the book about?

Fiction, nonfiction? Mystery, science, dinosaurs or bunnies, or both? Is this where you figure out the tone of the the type of story arc you need. I like books that teach a message, and my daughter likes mysteries. What does your child love?

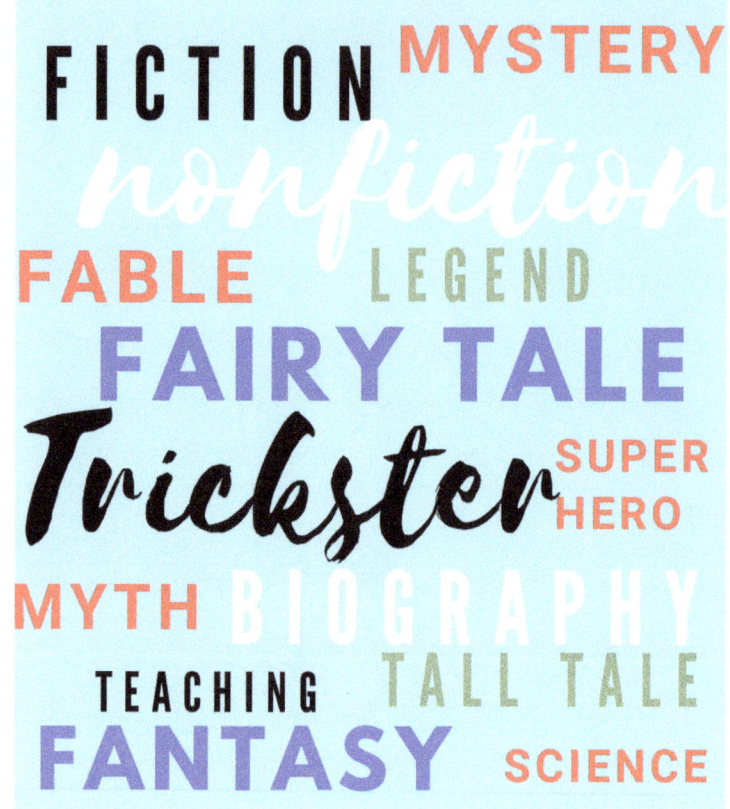

Author Page

Pros and Cons

The pros: I think its a great way to teach kids about how people perceive them and how they want to be known. Show an example from a book. This should be a positive experience. It also fills a page.

The cons: it fills a page, maybe you need that Page? Maybe your child is struggling with self esteem. Don't force it, but maybe write up a positive example and see if that helps? In the end, let your child decide.

Outline

It's not first, but it's in step one for a reason.

This is the time to brainstorm. You both know the type of book and the genre, so now let's get some more details down. A picture book is 300-750 words, so an outline will do most of the heavy lifting for this book. Print the Outline and Story Arc pages (pages 13-14), and have your child fill them in. It's okay if you help, but try to let your child make the decisions. Once this is done you have the bones of the story complete.

Congratulations!
Now your child has taken the first real steps toward writing a book. There are lots of adults who don't make it this far!

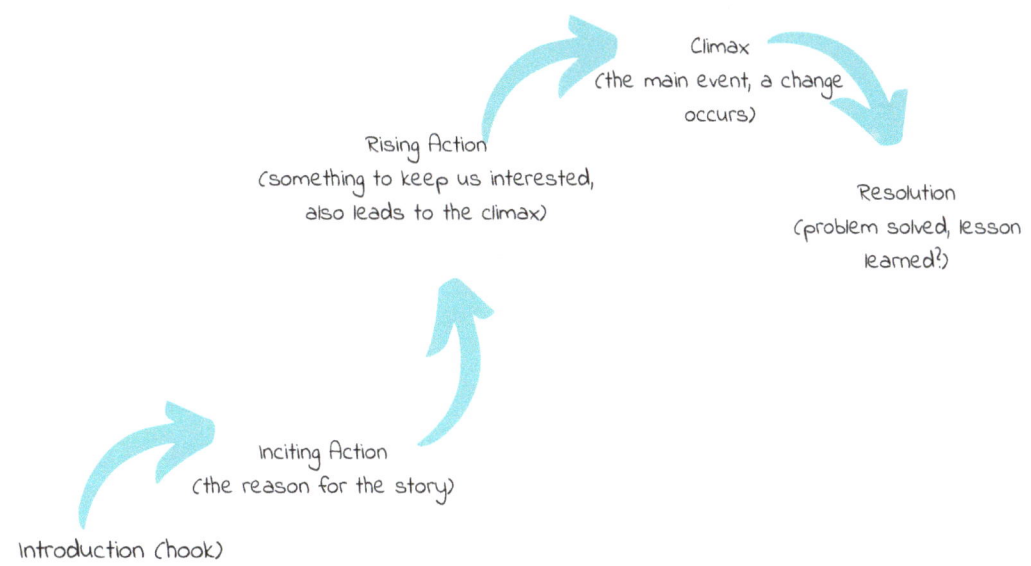

Number of Illustrations

A rough estimate

The story hasn't been finished yet, but its a good idea to get a rough estimate of what you will need. Look at the storyboards, and flip through some example books. You may notice that some books are all two page spreads, some are just cameo's like example A. Some are done with the words on one side and the illustration opposite, example B. And yet more books are mix. You don't have to decide now, but its something you will need to decide.

example A

example B

Print yourself
- 5x5
- half page
- 8.5 x 11

Printer
- 8x8
- 8.5x8.5
- 6x9
- 8x10
- 8.5 x 11

Size and Shape

Important detail

This almost went before outlining the book. Square or rectangle? It plays a huge role in the art. You don't want to create art in the wrong shape.

You can decide on final size later, but know your shape and create your art bigger. You can always shrink it later if needed. Just keep your details away from the edges so that nothing is lost.

Shannon L. Mokry | 12

Outline ⟶ _____

Genre

Plot summary _____
_____
_____
settings
_____
_____
plot summary
_____
_____

Setting _____
_____
_____
_____
main characters
Resolution
_____
_____
_____
_____
_____

conflict
Conflict _____
_____
resolution
_____
_____

Shannon L. Mokry | 13

Building Your Story
Planning for success

Introduction/Hook

_____
_____
_____
_____
_____
_____
_____
_____

Inciting Action

_____
_____
_____
_____
_____
_____
_____
_____

Rising Action

_____
_____
_____
_____
_____
_____
_____
_____

Climax

_____
_____
_____
_____
_____
_____
_____
_____

Falling Action

_____
_____
_____
_____
_____
_____
_____
_____

Conclusion

_____
_____
_____
_____
_____
_____
_____
_____

Introduction- This is where your audience meets your main character, or the story. It's your chance for your story to make its best impression.

Hook- One or more sentences that creates interest or excitement.

Inciting Action- The point or purpose that drives the rest of the story.

Rising Action- Is what gets you to the climax.

Climax- The most exciting part of the story.

Falling Action- Connects the Climax to the ending of the story.

Conclusion- The end of the story.

Story Arc

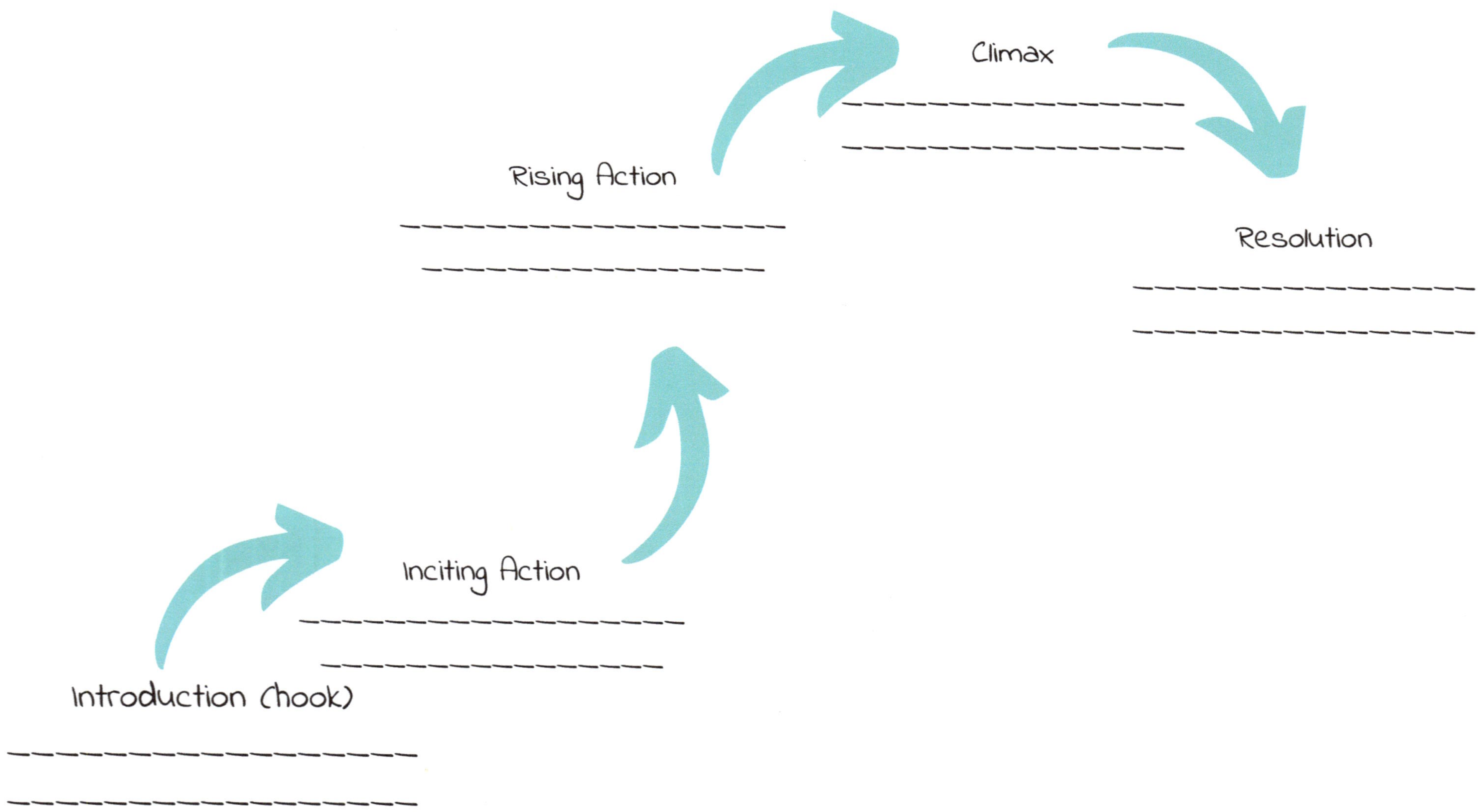

Resolution
_____

Climax
_____

Rising Action
_____

Inciting Action
_____

Introduction (hook)
_____

step 2

Write It

The Story

Every Great Book Starts with an Idea

You have the outline, you know the story arc, and now is the time to write the story. The complexity will depend a great deal on the age your child or class. My daughter struggles with reading and writing but tells amazing stories. So I typed while she talked. The first step was just getting it written (or typed). The end goal is 300-750 words. It's okay if the first draft is longer or shorter than this (although longer makes the process easier, so encourage descriptions and embellishment if needed at this point). Remember, its easier to trim a story than it's easier to add to it after your done.

Here are some helpful numbers:

- Picture Book – 300-750 words; the older the child the more words are acceptable
- Graphic Novel – less than 25 words per panel: no more than 200 words per page
- Young Reader Chapter Books – less than 10,000 words
- Middle Grade Chapter books – about 30,000 words

Shannon L. Mokry

Stuck?

Writer's Block

It's a real thing, even professionals get it. Not a problem for your child, skip ahead. For those of you struggling. You want this to be an amazing experience but your kid just says, "I don't know..." or some version of that. It can be discouraging for both of you. Thankfully, there are strategies to get around this. Some options include:

- Write down some choices and put them in a hat or bowl and pick one.
- Check out the story starters on the next page. These are just to get the creativity going.
- Other options are: Try a mad libs approach. Take a single line from a favorite book and change it. Either or both of these can spark some creativity.
- Offer to write it while your child dictates. I know mine gets so worked up in the process of writing that she can't think. It can be frustrating.

Story Starters

Don't feel like these are set in stone, change them up however you like!

The three little mice race across the kitchen...
- Why?
- What was on the other side of the kitchen?
- What was wrong with the side they were on?
- Were they friends or enemies?
- Was anyone else in the kitchen?

Mrs. Whiskers is stuck at the top of the tree. Can anyone save her?
- Is there a superhero around?
- If not a masked super hero, how about a real life hero like a firefighter?
- Is Mrs. Whiskers an animal or a person?
- Why is Mrs. Whiskers at the top of the tree?

"It's a bullfrog, get it away from me, get it away!"
- Who is screaming?
- Why?
- Is there anyone else in the scene?
- What's wrong with bullfrogs?

The clock struck midnight and the merry knight knew he had to get away from the party before...
- Before what?
- Why?
- What fairytale does this remind you of?
- Who else might be at the party?

It was almost dawn when she felt herself transform into a...
- A what?
- Get Creative! Was 'she' a cat that turned into a human?
- Is there anyone else around?
- Has this happened before?

step 3
Rewrite and Edit

Your Child is a Genius

Improving Perfection

Remember back when I told you that the outline and story arc will write most of the story for you? Then you learned how hard it was to fill in the details and still end up where you wanted to go? Well, now you're faced with a rewrite and the child doesn't want to do it. "It's perfect," says the child. Or maybe you think it's perfect. Let me ask you some questions. Did you fit it into the 300-750 words I told you about? If it's too long, you need to trim it up; if it's too short, you need more details.

Remember, if it's worth doing, then it's worth putting a little more effort into. I remember when I was in school and college, we always did at least two revisions, and I can tell you that it was ALWAYS worth my time.

Now as I publish children's books, I can tell you I STILL revise and rewrite, often 10-20 times before I feel it's good enough.

Here are some tips to get you started.

Read It Out Loud

From Start to Finish

If you trip over saying it, then readers will trip over reading it.

Find an Audience

Otherwise Knows as Beta Readers

This is your test audience. Is there something they loved? Something they hated? Was anything confusing?

Can the Art Show It?

The Words and the Art Work Together

Not everything said needs to be pictured, but the words and the art need create a complete story.

2 for 1
Complements and Fix Its

We are talking about a child's writing. Make sure you are encouraging. Give two complements for ever one fix it suggestion. Remember, its a suggestion. Your child must decide to fix it or leave it.

Shannon L. Mokry | 23

Rewrites, Edits, and Page Breaks

Wait, What?

You just did all the rewrites and edits, did you think about page breaks?

Take a moment and look at a picture book. How did they decide what words to put on what page?

- Natural pauses in the story
- Change of scene or speaker
- Too many words on one page. Read it out again and see if you can exaggerate a word to accommodate a page turn. AAANNDD.... page turn...

I know you think your done now. It's time to make your art and put it all together right? Nope, now you need to edit again.

Line Editing

This is not the same as the rewriting and editing you did before. This is strictly for finding typos, grammar mistakes, and punctuation mistakes. Outsource this step. Believe me, it's worth it! You don't have to spend money on this. Instead think of all your friends and family, do you know any of these people? Ask one or two to give it look over.

- English teacher
- A college student that loves to read
- A professional that loves to correct memos

Now the story is ready to pair up with your art.

step 4
Illustration Time

Let's Talk Art

Is your child a budding illustrator, or still stuck on stick figures?

When it comes to picture books, the art is just as important as the words. It's true, the two things need to work together. With that said, you have some homework. You need to go to the library or a book store and really look at a variety of picture books. Take notes. What did you find?

I'll tell you what I found. ALL KINDS OF ART. Some of it I liked, some of it I thought "What was the publisher thinking?"

Don't worry about how well you think your child draws. This is a reminder of today's skills. A snapshot in time. Embrace that, encourage it, and remember that childhood doesn't need negativity. Where you see a mess, other children will relate. Of course you can encourage the best. You can even make requests. However, remember my caution during the writing process: it's not your book, and your relationship with your child is worth more than your version of perfection.

My Child is an Artist
This book is really about showcasing my child's art

If this section describes your child then you might skip this section.
All your child needs is the page cuts so that they can determine what art to draw, paint, or even photograph.

For everyone else, keep going.

My Child Loves Art, But...
So your child loves art, but isn't as skilled as Picasso

That is okay too! Think of this book as a snapshot in time. This is not the place for your inner art critique. This is a place to make your child feel special. If you just can't bring yourself to use your child's art (it's at the stage that you can't recognize what it's a scribble of), let's be honest you knew that when you started this project.

You have two options: collaborate, you do the art, your child does the words, or pull out the clip art and let them design with someone else's art. Think of it as digital sticker art, or a digital collage.

Forging Ahead

My child's art is somewhere in the middle

You can use or lose my suggestions, but here is one technique...have your child make the backdrops, think of them as a stage on which the story will be set. Then make each element.

After that is complete, you will need to digitize the art. A home scanner will work, just be aware that you need a program to adjust the color balance. If the art is to big for your scanner then you have two options. Option one is to photograph the art with a digital camera. Option two is call around to camera stores looking for one that can scan or photograph the art for you. Be aware that option two can get pricey.

This is where most kids are. My daughter's art improves every time she draws and redraws something, but her patience for that is limited.

Start by brainstorming image ideas that go with the page breaks you have already figured out. Make a list of elements that need to be included on each page.

Also, take a minute and talk about backgrounds. How many different backgrounds do you need?
It is helpful if you can limit the number of backgrounds needed to 1-3.

step 5

Finishing Touches

Putting it all together

Learning Basic Graphic Design

What we are going to talk about here is how to make a visually appealing image using your independently drawn or painted elements. Since this is a keepsake, you can even allow your child to use clip art. What you will need:

Adobe Elements
www.Canva.com Account
Your child's art (either scanned or photographed)

Another resource that is helpful:
https://www.canva.com/colors/color-palette-generator/

Pick a template below. When you click on it, you should be taken to your Canva account.

5x5 Print at Home Template - https://smarturl.it/booktemplate1
8x8 template - https://smarturl.it/booktemplate2
11x8.5 template - https://smarturl.it/booktemplate3
8.5x11 template - https://smarturl.it/booktemplate4

I suggest you make a copy and rename before moving on to the next step

Building your Book

With Complete illustrations (skip to the next page if your building your illustrations)

Getting to know Canva

My templates are designed to have the illustrations on one side and the words on the opposite side. Please don't feel like you are stuck with this design. I chose these for simplicity. Take a moment to learn to navigate Canva.

- Find the File link on the top left. Click on the file link, select copy and save.
- After you make your copy, go up to the top right and click on the name of the file and rename it with your book's name.
- Everything within the template is changeable. If you accidently delete something, use the back arrow on the top left.
- You'll use the upload link along the left side to upload your illustrations. Make sure they are in .jpg or .png format.
- Use the text link along the left side to add a text box. Or click on the text box that is already there, delete what is there and your own words.
- You can change the color of a page by clicking the page, then looking at the top left for a little colored box. Click the box and it will give you color options on the left.
- You can change your text color by clicking the text box and looking for an A with a rainbow below it, along the top bar.

Once you have built your book

You will want to click on the download button on the far right. Make sure you select the right download format. To print, either yourself or using a printer, click on PDF PRINT and download (if you need any other format I'll note it on page 31). Make sure to delete any pages that you don't want in you final book.

Building a Page

For those using the layering technique.

Set Up Your Book

Pick your template and set up the basics of your book.

- Get to know Canva
- Open your template and rename it
- Pick your color scheme and set up your template
- Insert your text
- Insert your backdrop illustrations

Get Your Images Ready

This is the hardest part. You need to remove all the white background on each element of created for your illustrations.

- Canva has a background remover
- I use Photoshop
- Save your final image as .png)if you save as .jpg it will put the white background back on the image)

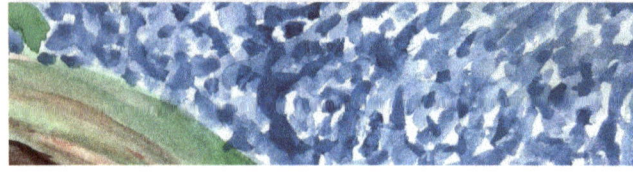

Add Your Layers

This is a great time to introduce the depth of field concept.

- Layer the back stuff first.
- The back items should be the smallest
- Each layer should be slightly larger than the last layer
- Be sure to have a focal point

Balance and Purpose

Every element in the illustration should have a purpose. Remind your child that the illustrations works with the words. For example, they can:

- Tell part of the story
- Support the story
- Give unwritten details

Shannon L. Mokry| 32

step 6

Covers

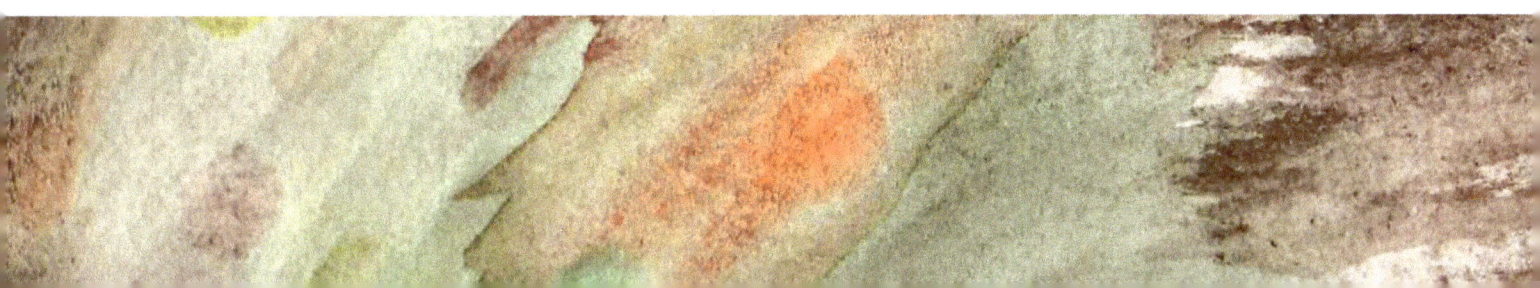

Making a Cover

Do you judge a book by its cover?

Let's be honest, we all judge a book by its cover. It is the first thing that grabs our attention. It determines if we pick it up or pass it by.

Thankfully, this book will be well read and loved no matter what the cover looks like, but that doesn't mean you should ignore it.

My thoughts on the cover go like this:
- Can we use the Title Page? Yes! Just don't forget to make a back cover. (You can make it using the same template, just don't download it with the rest of the book).
- Does my child want to design a special cover? If yes, then open a new document with the same sizing as the interior template and create a front and a back.
- Some printing companies may have special requirements. Now is the time to take a moment before creating the cover to pick your printer, Companies like Shutterfly have preset covers, while IngramSpark have a template you can use. More on printers on the next page.

Whatever you decide, that is the last step!
Congratulations!

What Now?

Comparing your print options

Local printer

I won't be able to list all the local printers out there. This is a list of national chain companies, but I suggest looking up local printers online.

- www.staples.com: offers coil-binded books or saddle-stitch binding
- www.officedepot.com: offers hardcover photo b (download pages individually as .png files), saddle-stitch or square edged booklet. Check the site or sizes available.

There are many more companies that do this. Take a few moments to do an internet search for printing companies in your area (or the closest large city).

Online

Online printers will have the most options but don't support your local economy and usually have the longest wait time before you can hold your finished book in your hands. That doesn't mean it isn't the best option. For many sizes and options, online ordering might be the only option.

- www.canva.com offers printing for books in certain sizes. That makes it easy. Click the three dots up next to the download button and scroll to the print options.
- www.shutterfly.com: 8x8 only, but it offers both hardback and softbound (download individual pages as .jpg)
- www.ingramspark.com: the most options. Choose print only (not distribution). This option is meant for professionals but can also be used for smaller projects.

There are many more options, but most require large orders and are meant for professional publishing.

thank you

I had a great deal of fun making this guide and testing it with my own daughter. I hope you found it useful in your own journey. If you did, then here are a few things you can do to help support me on my journey.

#1 - Consider giving me a testimonial to use, feedback is greatly appreciated. send testimonials to:info@sillygeesepublishing.com

#2 - Add one or more of my books to your child's library.

#3 - Share your child's finished book on social media with the hashtag #mychildwroteabook

#4 - Then follow the hashtag to cheer other children on!

Sillygeese Publishing, llc

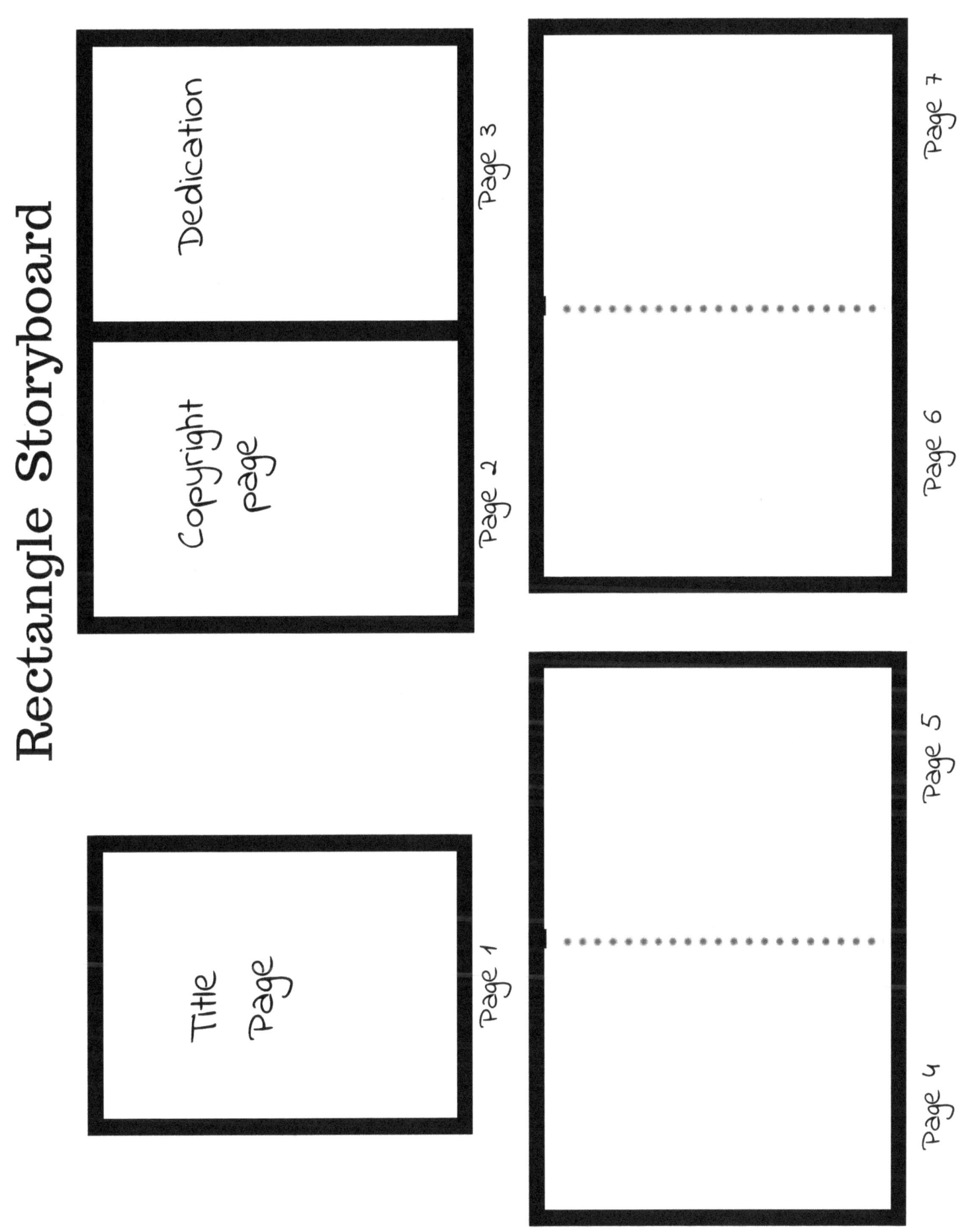

Rectangle Storyboard

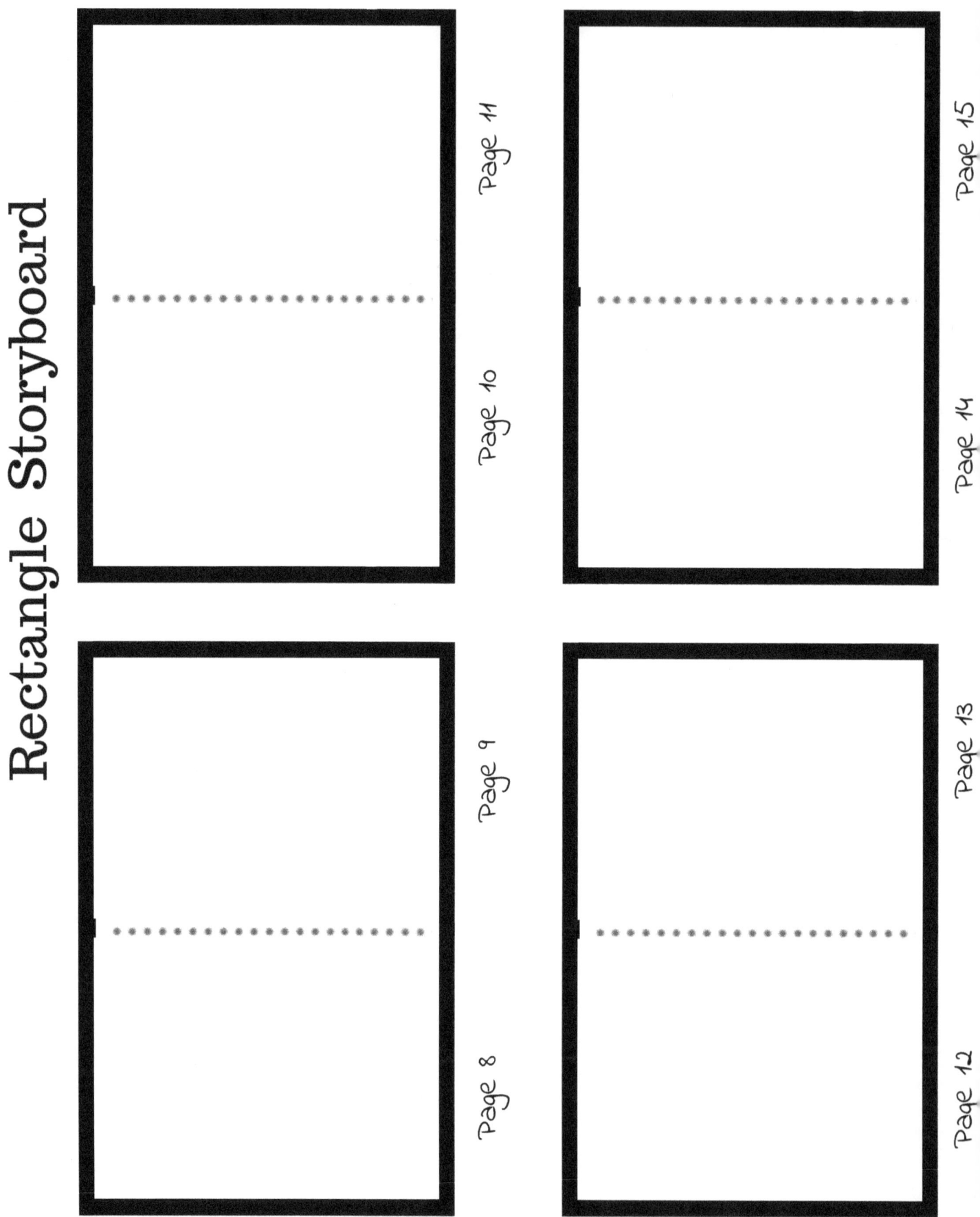

Rectangle Storyboard

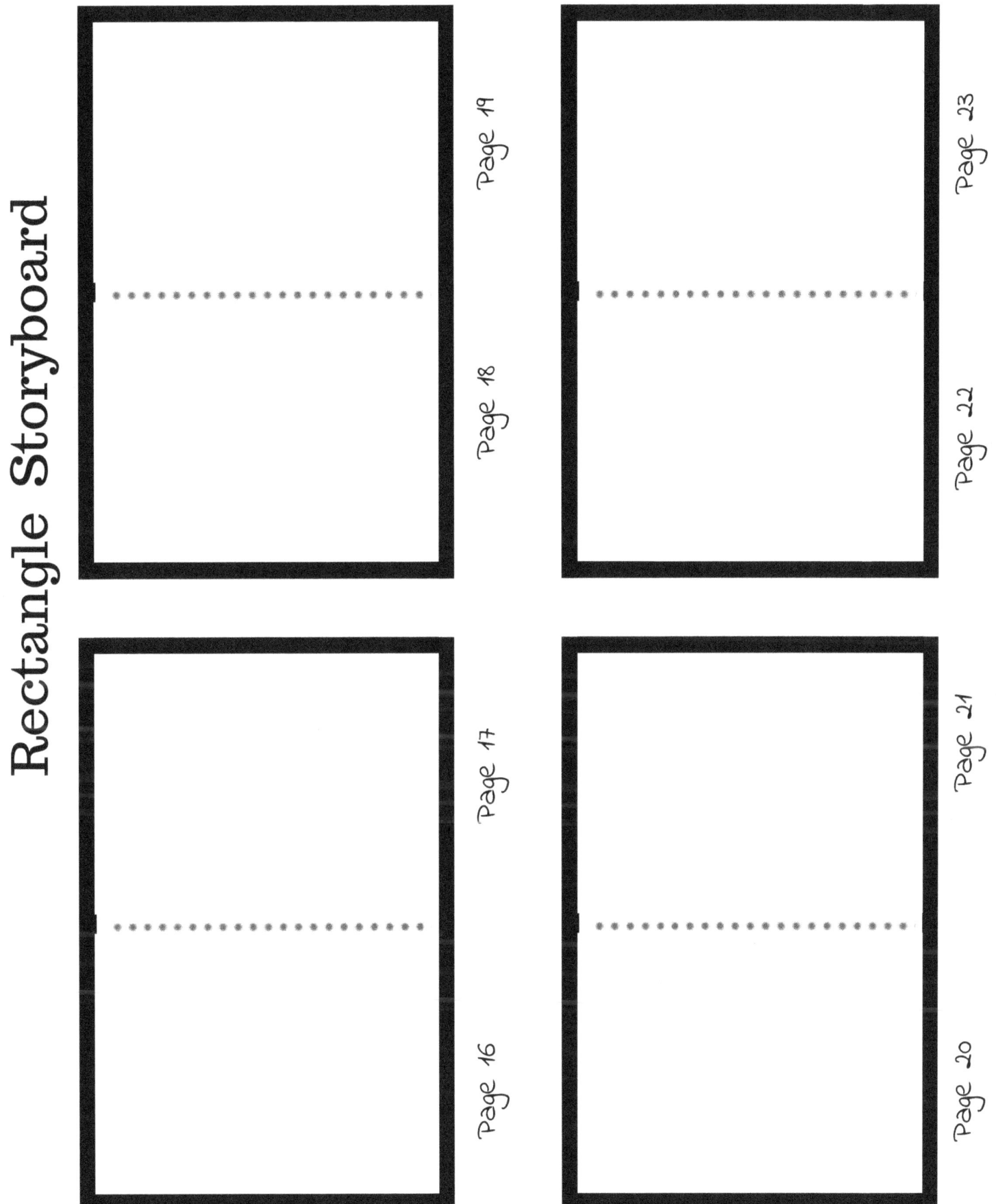

Rectangle Storyboard

Notes _____

Page 24
about the author?

inside cover

Shannon L. Mokry

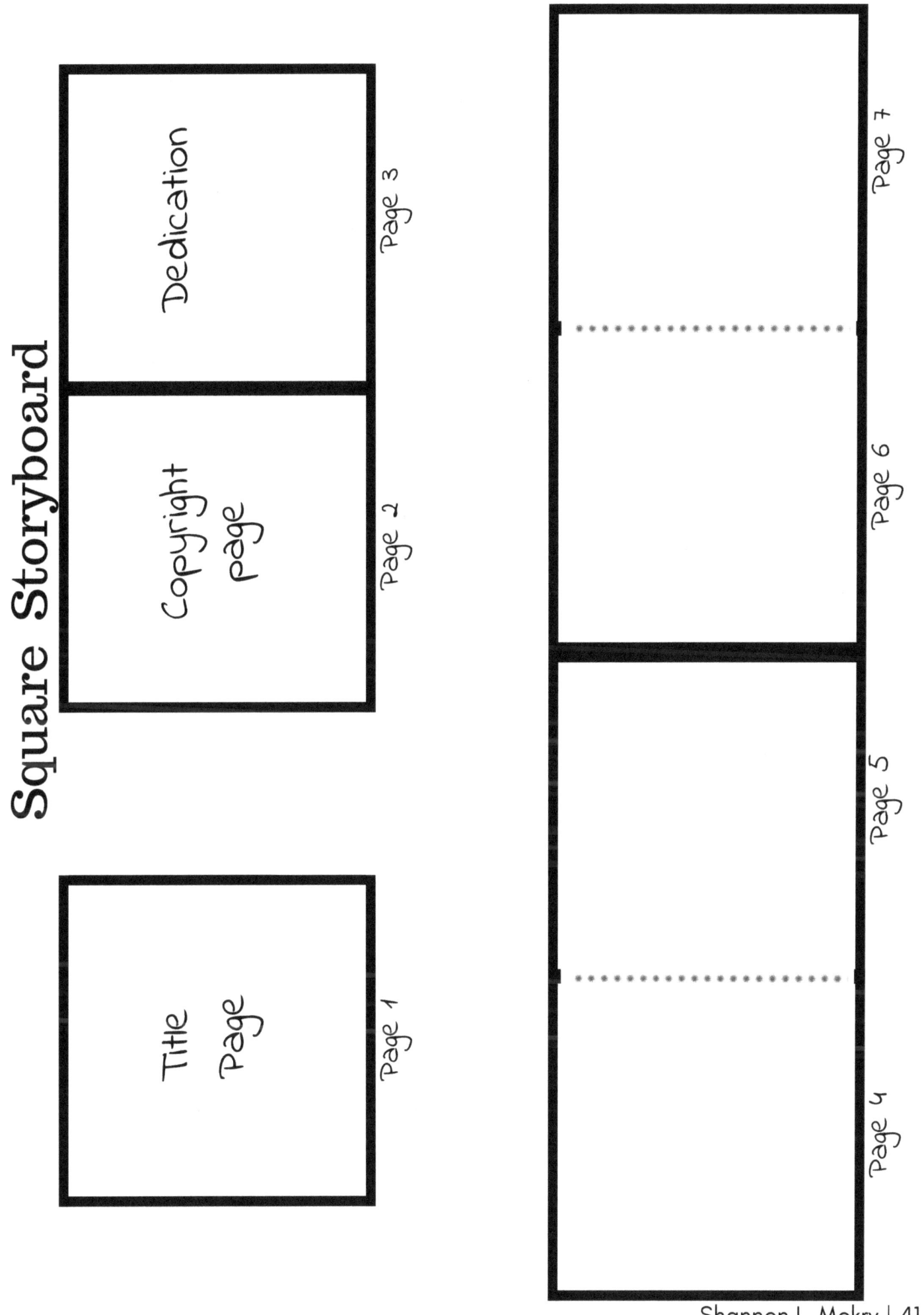

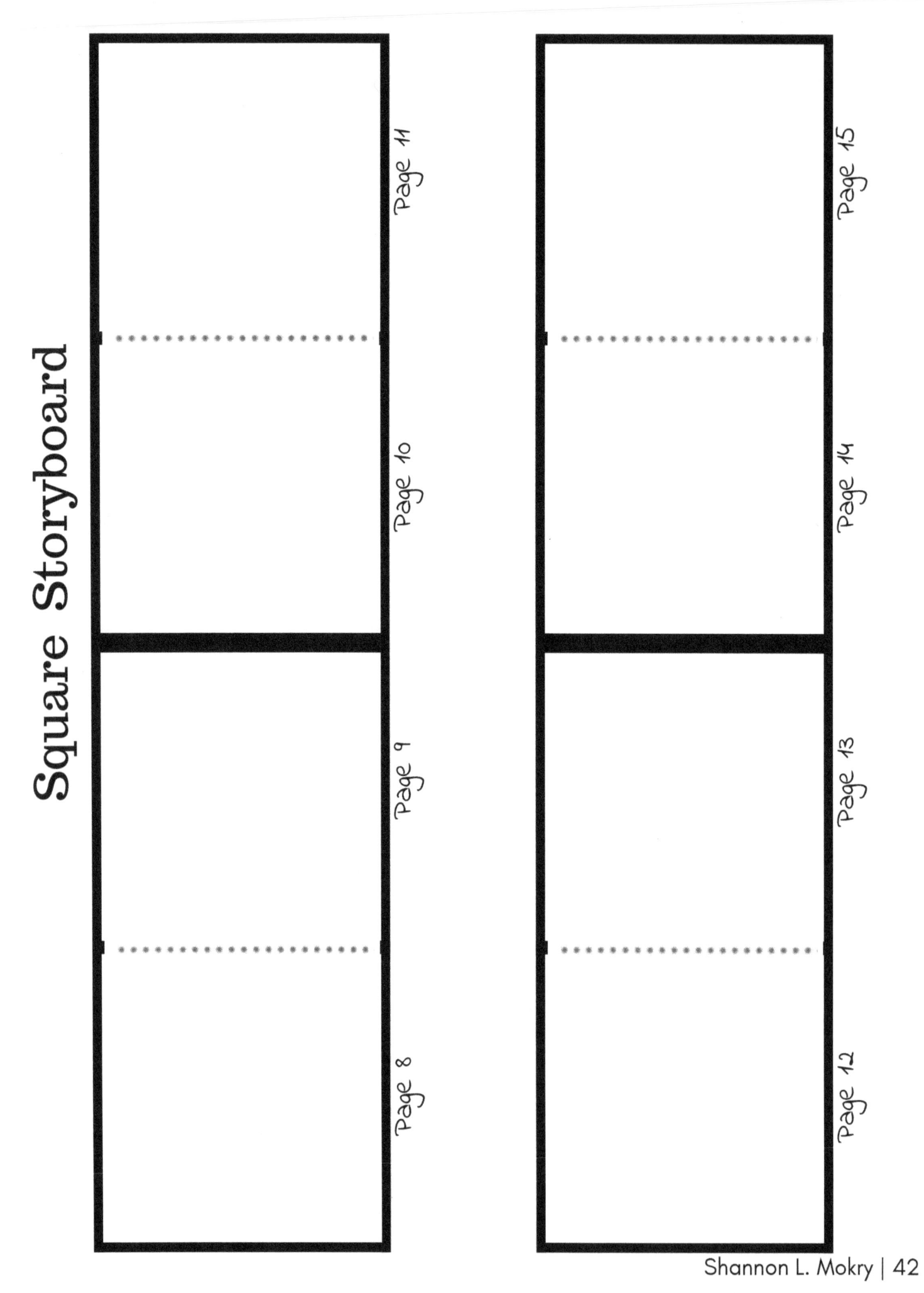

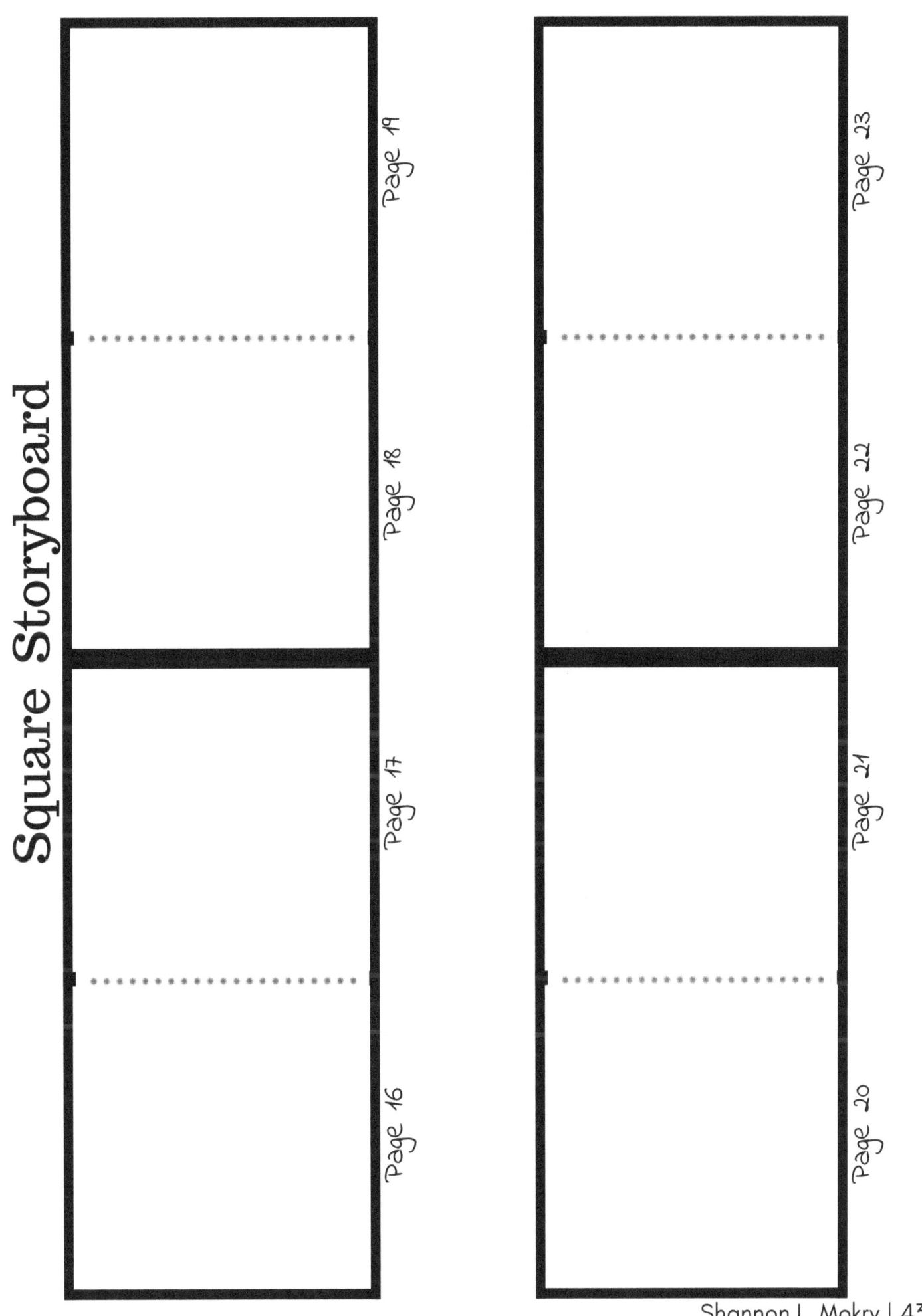

Square Storyboard

Notes

inside cover

Page 24
about the author?